FROM·THE·LIBRARY·OF

place pawprint here...

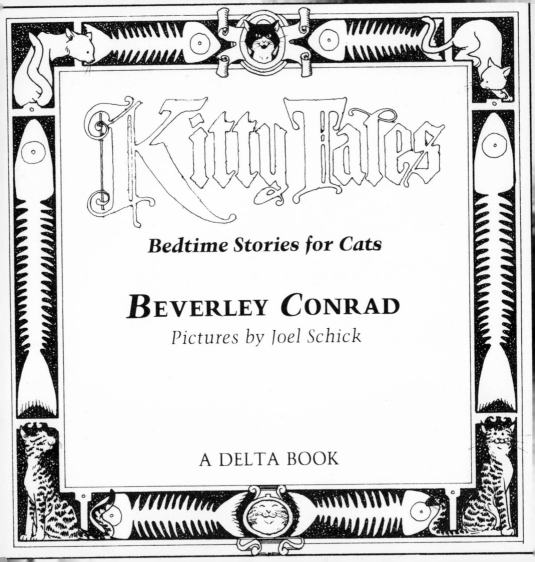

Kitty Tales

Bedtime Stories for Cats

BEVERLEY CONRAD

Pictures by Joel Schick

A DELTA BOOK

A DELTA BOOK
Published by
Dell Publishing Co., Inc.
1 Dag Hammarskjold Plaza
New York, New York 10017

Delta ® TM 755118,
Dell Publishing Co., Inc.
Printed in the United States of America
First Printing—March 1980

Library of Congress Cataloging in Publication Data

Conrad, Beverley, 1950-
Kitty tales.

(A Delta book)
CONTENTS: The cat who spat the golden hairball.—
The three kitty cats' fluff.—Duchess and the pea.—
The three little kitties.—[etc.]
1. Cats—Anecdotes, facetiae, satire, etc.
I. Schick, Joel. II. Title.
PN6231.C23C66   813'.54   79-28397

ISBN 0-440-51458-4

Dedicated to Stash and Cat

Dedicated to Stash and her fourteen years of loyal mouse-batting, affection-giving service to the Conrad family, and to Cat, named Cat because he was one, wherever he is.

TABLE OF CONTENTS

Introduction

Cats have always been revered for their independence, their playfulness, and their renowned curiosity. Now you can *safely* satisfy your cat's curiosity about life with *Kitty Tales*.

No doubt you have spent hours calling your cat only to have him sneak away or look at you with disinterest. Cats have to have something to amuse them, and once you show yours that you have *Kitty Tales*, he will come racing to you, happy that you will read to him. It helps of course if you open a can of cat food when you pick up the book. This will be necessary for only a little while, however, as your cat will soon become accustomed to his new toy.

With *Kitty Tales* your pet will have a newfound interest in life. No longer will he while away the hours hanging out in alleyways with his friends. No longer will he just lie about the house snorting catnip. Au contraire! Once he learns what life among cats is all about, he may even express an interest in getting a job—perhaps as a mouse trapper in the Yukon.

As for the lady cats, *Kitty Tales* will amuse them on Saturday nights, eliminating useless hours spent staring and howling out windows. They will listen with ardor as you read stories of romance and adventure. They will swish their tails at the exciting parts, pouncing occasionally on an imaginary rat. They will purr at the happy endings.

Read in a soft voice. Kitty cats like this. And let your cat bat the pages as you read. He is just trying to see how the stories end. Before long you too will be batting at the pages as curious as your cat about the stories' outcome—at which point you and your kitty can happily chant this motto together: Good reading for good breeding.

And if you hear strange noises coming from your cat's bed in the middle of the night, it is probably only your cat reading his little book to himself. After all, you are the one who needs the flashlight under the covers to read at night. He can see in the dark.

Acatin and the Magic Lamp

NCE UPON A TIME in a distant country lived a Persian named Acatin. He was a cat.

One day Acatin was just catting around near the seashore looking for fish and various things to eat. One of his habits was poking around the seashore, as that was where the best fish, ready for eating, hung out.

Poking and sniffing, around and around he went, searching for the tastiest fish left on the shore that day.

13

Soon he spied a large golden fish much different from the rest. It had *14K gold-filled* stamped on its bottom, and the oil that he smelled was not of cod but of patchouli.

"What a weird fish," Acatin mewed. He began to stare and pounced on it. Once. Twice. Thrice he pounced, wondering what could be the nature of this weird fish.

On the third pounce he heard a whoosh of wind, and suddenly, above the strange golden fish, which was not a fish at all but a weird lamp, floated a cloud with eyes and whiskers.

"YEOW!" he screeched, and all the fur on his back stood on end. The cloud purred.

"Hello, Acatin," it began. "You are inventive and a kind purr-sian cat, and for letting me out of my lamp I shall grant you three wishes."

Acatin, being a rather excitable cat when something surprised him, shrieked again, "YEOW!"

"Stop that, Acatin," the thing in the cloud purred. "You were the curious one who pounced on my lamp.

Now you are the lucky one, for you shall have three wishes. Shall we begin?"

Acatin paced. Then he glared. He was good at glaring. He crept around and around the strange creature with the eyes and whiskers. Then he mewed, "I wish I had a fish." He figured he'd start out with something simple to see whether this wishing thing was true.

Immediately a large fillet of flounder flipped down from the sky and landed right at Acatin's paws.

"Next?"

"I will think for a moment," mewed Acatin, busily filling his face. "I see that you mean what you say, and therefore I must carefully consider my next two wishes."

When Acatin finished eating his fish, he lay back and casually picked at his teeth with a fine bone while he considered his next move. Acatin was enterprising as well as inventive, curious, and kind.

"I wish for all the catnip in the world," he said. And immediately he was surrounded by all the catnip in the entire world, which was an enormous amount. Acatin

wondered for a moment if that was really such a good wish, but sniffing it all over, he decided that it was the best stuff he could come up with in the way of wishes. It was certainly plentiful. He sniffed at it some more, then out of the clear blue he got it into his head to start batting it around. Catnip does that to cats. He grew giddy and before long was giggling and batting and floating around in such a manner as to arouse the attention of other cats in the neighboring seaside resorts. As soon as they sniffed Acatin's catnip, they too started giggling and floating and batting the catnip around. Soon the noise from these cats aroused the attention of more cats. And they came! And then more cats! And more cats!

Clearly this was a rather silly wish. Poor Acatin could do nothing, however, as he was too busy batting and giggling and floating.

A major news service heard of the plight of all these batting, giggling, floating cats and went to check it out. The news anchorcat began: "We are standing in front of fifteen thousand batting, giggling, floating cats who seem to have been affected by an overabundance of cat-nip. We will now try to interview Acatin, the cat who allegedly perpetrated this event. "Acatin," he said, hold-ing the tiny microphone aloft, "tell us what happened..."

"Wow, man," began Acatin. "Like there was this weird fish . . ."

"You heard it all right here, all you cats. A 'weird fish' has done this . . ."

"No, man," Acatin purred. "It was eyes and whiskers . . ."

"Weird whiskers, cats. Acatin says that weird whiskers . . ."

"No, man, like you got it all wrong...Oh, man, I wish I could get rid of this catnip stuff and . . ." *Poof!* and *whoosh!* it was *gone!* And immediately all the fifteen thousand cats landed on their sixty-thousand feet.

Acatin quickly buried the strange lamp that looked like a fish but wasn't lest one of these cats should find it and make the same silly wish he had made. Then he covered the spot with some special wood shavings—the kind that will eliminate odors—to disguise the patchou-li oil smell.

The story nevertheless made it into the *National Cat*, which specializes in stories of an odd and sensational nature, and soon some cats interested in capitalizing on the phenomenon of the batting, giggling, floating cats began creating and distributing certain paraphernalia pertaining to weird cats. And although all the weird cats claim that there is no more catnip in the world, there certainly are a lot of stores that sell related products.

The Cat Who Spat the Golden Hairball

 NCE UPON A TIME there was a beautiful little kitty who had, of all things, a coat of the finest spun gold. She was the envy of all the other lady cats in the land. She was also the heartthrob of all the male cats.

The beautiful little kitty's name was Goldy. For a while it was Blondie, but Goldy actually suited her better.

Each morning little but amazingly heavy Goldy would groom her coat. She would lick it, shining the pure spun gold until it shone like the sun. Occasionally she swallowed a strand or two, as cats will do, but no harm ever came of that. Again as cats will do, she occasionally spat a hairball or two—and naturally they were solid gold.

Of course Goldy became the envy of all the lady cats in the land when she began spitting twenty-four-karat hairballs. They knew that if Max, King of the Alley, should hear about her, they would surely not have a hairball's chance in whatever against Goldy. Surely, Max would marry her!

The lady cats called a meeting. Every lady cat in all the land was invited except Goldy—who was so busy making earrings out of her whiskers she did not care.

"We have a problem," meowed a magnificent Persian cat who, alas, had nothing but a plain fur coat. "Max will surely marry Goldy, for he is an enterprising cat who is swayed by things like solid-gold hairballs."

"Stop him! Stop him!" shrieked all the other cats in except one. She was rather scrawny, but she looked wise.

"Mew," she said. Immediately one thousand cat eyes were upon her. "No reason to worry," she mewed. "He is a rich cat, that is true, for he is king. But let him court Goldy. Soon enough the romance will end." Then she scurried up a utility pole and was gone.

"She's crazy!" yowled most of the cats.

"But wise!" mewed yet another cat. "Evidently she knows something of the ways of doting male cats."

Sure enough, Max heard of Goldy and her spun-gold coat and subsequent twenty-four-karat by-products and went to find her, court her, and marry her.

"Goldy! Oh, my beautiful Goldy!" he howled, trying to sound very much in love. "I have come to court you and be nice to you. Then I will marry you." Max was a rather up-front cat.

"Okay," mewed Goldy, who did not have the vaguest idea what he was howling about, but she was bored with grooming and shining and making jewelry.

"Oh, goody!" howled Max, rubbing his little paws together. Soon all her golden hair balls will be mine, he thought slyly.

"Now what?" purred Goldy, smiling naively into Max's puss. "You said you would be nice to me. May I request individual niceties?"

"Me-oh, okay," mewed Max, slightly confused. When he had said he would be nice to her, he meant something along the lines of dinner out at his dish.

"I think I should like to go to Kitty's Paradise!" mewed Goldy. "It is a place that grooms lady cats, and I should like to be truly beautiful once and for all, for I am sick of grooming myself."

"Me-oh," mewed Max. His plan wasn't working as he had expected.

Woe to Max! At Kitty's Paradise, Goldy had herself a grand old time. She was washed and permed, coiffed and curled, and before long her twenty-four-karat coat resembled a Brillo pad that had scrubbed a mountain of pots.

"I feel pretty! Oh, so pretty! I feel pretty! A kitty! And bri-i-i-i-i-ght!" she caterwauled. Max could hear her coming. "Look, Max!" Goldy screeched, so happy that she could hardly contain herself. "Never again will I have to sit and groom my obnoxious 24-karat coat. Why, I shall never have to brush my coat again! In fact, I shall never *be able* to brush my coat again!" With that she jumped into the air to show Max just how springy her new coat was.

"Aughhh!" screeched Max. "I think I am needed in my alleyway," he mewed and at once beat a hasty retreat from Goldy's yard.

Needless to say, Goldy never heard from Max, King of the Alley, again. Max was again "available," and the lady cats in the neighborhood got another chance to snare him. Goldy gave up her hobby of making jewelry and was last seen running feverishly around the inside of a large pot, screeching, "Send down more soap! I think the pot is starting to shine!" She is very happy.

The Three Kitty Cats' Fluff

NCE UPON A TIME there lived three absolutely gorgeous cats who had absolutely gorgeous coats. They were part Persian, part Angora, and underneath all their fluff, part cat, though the last part was hardly distinguishable at times.

Puffy, Buffy, and Stuffy had jobs in the city as rat-catchers. In days gone by this used to be a menial job, but ever since the invention of the mousetrap having a real live cat to chase after real live mice and rats had been a status symbol.

Puffy, Buffy, and Stuffy each worked different shifts. They went to work at different hours, chased rats at different hours, and came home at different hours. In short they strived to be individuals.

Bright and early one fine day Puffy packed his little jar of milk and his little rubber mouse with a squeaker into his little brown bag and set off for work. His little rubber mouse was about as active as a sleeping rat, and though chasing it was not the greatest sport in the world, it was good practice. On the way to work he spied the sign that said "Troll Bridge One Mile. Please Slow Down" and knew that soon he would come to that very bridge. He was not worried. He slowed his pace gradually, blinking one eye as he approached the bridge to signal that he was about to pull over.

Now the keeper of the troll gate at the troll bridge was named Choo. (Many trolls are named Choo, but unless you've met one, you wouldn't know this.)

Choo was a weird troll who had lived under the bridge ever since he'd decided one day that he should. On that day, returning from a road trip that had taken him on most major highways, he'd announced that many of those highways were "troll roads" and henceforth he would act as other trolls did, collecting money from everyone passing over his bridge before allowing them to continue down the road.

Choo the troll had a way of demonstrating his authority so that no one disputed him and everyone automatically dug into their little pouches for coins as they neared his bridge.

So when Puffy came to the bridge, Choo jumped up and held out his hand.

"Pay troll," he said matter-of-factly.

"Okay," said Puffy just as matter-of-factly.

Alas! Poor Puffy had not one coin in his little pouch. How could he have been so silly as to forget his coin for Choo? Perhaps, Puffy thought suddenly, Choo would accept a trade.

"Here," he said. "How about this lovely little rubber mouse with a squeaker? It is great company!"

"Not on your nine lives!" yelled Choo. "I still have that rat you gave me a month ago, the one that was supposed to be 'only sleeping.' There he sits in the maze I built him, and he has not even passed Start yet!"

"Alas!" cried Puffy. "Then I cannot pay you."

"Pull over!" yelled Choo into his loudspeaker. Choo

did have a certain air about him. And poor Puffy pulled over and was put into a cage under the bridge.

Later the same day Buffy readied himself for work. He too packed his little jar of milk, his rubber mouse, and a bunch of freshly cut catnip to bat during his break. Sure enough, there was Choo waiting at the troll bridge.

"Pay troll," he said just as matter-of-factly as before.

"I'll owe it to you," said Buffy, also matter-of-factly.

"You can't owe it to me," whined Choo. "That's not how this troll stuff works." And he tried it again. "Pay troll."

"Alas!" cried Buffy. "I lost all my coins in a card game last night. We were playing old maid for cats, and I kept getting stuck with the Queen of Spayeds! Oh, woe is me! What shall I do? I cannot pay the troll."

"Same thing as the rest of the cats who don't pay— you shall go to the cage." Choo flicked a switch that set a red light spinning and a siren screaming (Choo was into gadgets), and Buffy was thrown into the cage with Puffy.

Just before midnight, for that was when his shift began, Stuffy packed together his dinner in his little lunch pail. He too packed some milk, some toys, and a whole bunch of tissues to keep all his toys from rattling around.

As he approached the troll bridge Stuffy flicked the switch that turned on his taillights. Stuffy was a stickler for detail and steered himself over to Choo, making little putting noises to add to the effect.

"Pay troll," said Choo.

"Okay," said Stuffy. Then he flipped a coin into Choo's basket.

"Go on," said Choo, flicking the switch that turned on the green light.

All of a sudden what did Stuffy hear but a great mewing, howling, and screeching from below the bridge!

"What goes on here?" Stuffy howled with as much authority as Choo had ever had. "Have you captured my poor little basket mates Puffy and Buffy?"

"Well, sure," said Choo. "They could not pay the troll."

"Then I shall pay for them," said Stuffy and pulled his pocket inside out. It was empty, and he had not one coin left to free poor Puffy and Buffy. What ever would he do? Stuffy puffed into a ball to think for a moment, then sprang to his paws.

"Alas," he began. "Without poor Puffy and Buffy the city will certainly fall into ruin. Why, what would happen if that innovative flute player from Hamlin shows up? It would be so sad, so very sad. For years inventors have been trying to invent a better mousetrap. They will miss poor Puffy and Buffy, for they were the best. How sad . . ."

"Stop it! Stop it!" cried Choo. "You are breaking my all-too trollish heart! Oh, boo hoo hoo hoo!"

"Here," said Stuffy, and he handed Choo a tissue. Choo took it and blew his nose and dried his eyes. Then he looked at the tissue.

"My goodness," he sniffed. "For years I have always thought of this stuff as worthless paper, but it is certainly valuable when one needs it. Henceforth this worthless paper shall be used as currency. We shall call it"— he thought for a moment—"worthless paper currency!" Then he said to Stuffy, "If you give me some of this stuff, I shall release Puffy and Buffy." And Stuffy did. And Choo did.

Now that might be the end of *that* story, but it is hardly the end of the *whole* story. There are certain people who remember the tale of the three cats and the kindness of Choo the troll and how he allowed Puffy and Buffy to go free. When these people are near cats with absolutely gorgeous coats and lots of fluff, they become nostalgic and weep a little and sniff. They remember the troll and speak his name, saying over and over again "Ah! Choo! Ah! Choo!" And people nearby, as if on command, will hand them a piece of the worthless paper currency, which is really worth all the coins in the world—if one needs it.

Duchess and the Pea

NCE UPON A TIME in a land some-
where near the Catskills lived a
beautiful little kitty cat named
Duchess. She was named Duchess
because of her somewhat royal lineage.

As is the custom with little kitties, especially those
of fine and fastidious breeding, a grand ball was to be
given in her honor. The ball would herald her arrival
into the world of grown-up cats, and from that day on

she would be allowed to meet many handsome cats of similar fine and fastidious breeding.

Woe to poor Duchess, however. A certain catty lady cat who wrote a column on cats decided to do a splash on Duchess.

Not because it was particularly right but because it would sell magazines, the catty old cat found an early picture of Duchess. Snipping carefully here and there, she pasted the picture of Duchess on top of another picture in such a way, shall we say, as to mislead the public.

The following week there it was: Duchess's photo plastered on the cover of *Photocat Magazine* with poor Duchess crouching next to an old garbage can in an old alleyway with mice and rats scurrying to and fro and an old shoe flying out a window at her. Beneath the photograph was the headline: IS DUCHESS REALLY A DUCHESS? OR IS SHE JUST ANOTHER FRAUDIE CAT? FIND OUT...The page number followed.

Poor Duchess! Whatever would she do? Why, her

grand coming-out party was approaching, and no fine cat would dance with her or court her if they did not believe that she was truly a duchess.

"What shall I do? What shall I do?" she cried, weeping little bitty tears into her little bitty paws—for she was a duchess and therefore not prone to wildcat outbursts. "What ever shall I do?"

Feeling sad and confused, she crept onto a window-sill. Sometimes it helped her to sit and stare.

What should she see coming up the walk to her house but a hundred cats, neighbor cats of hers, evidently coming to hear the dreadful story for themselves.

"Kitty litter! That's what it is!" she shrieked, slightly losing her well-bred cool. "How can you believe the litter printed in those magazines?" And once again she took to weeping.

All of a sudden a rather handsome and debonair cat, obviously of a rare yet unnamed breed, pranced and danced up to the front of the cat crowd, where he made this announcement: "You have come to see if Duchess is truly a duchess. I will prove to you that she is." Then he smiled a charming smile and disappeared.

Soon a Mack truck pulled up in front of the house, and the strange debonair cat jumped out.

"Here are one thousand mattresses from one thousand little cat beds," he said. "Here is a pea. Tonight I will place the pea under the stack of one thousand mattresses, and Duchess will sleep on top of them. If Duchess is really a duchess, the pea will affect her oddly. If she is not, it will not. I read about this method in a book once and it is known to work."

Duchess decided to go to bed immediately, since she knew it would take her half the night to reach the top mattress. Five hours later she curled up on the top mattress. The hundred neighborhood cats lay down to wait.

All night long they heard Duchess jumping around. She would stare at the mattress for a moment or two, then suddenly pounce on a spot that for all practical purposes was empty. All night she carried on like this.

And the following morning she was still carrying on.

When one of the hundred cats inquired why she was pouncing at nothing, the strange debonair cat appeared, smiled, and answered for her. 'Only a cat of truly fine and fastidious breeding would be able to feel a pea beneath all one thousand mattresses. Duchess cannot see it to pounce on it, but she pounces on the spot where she feels it."

The one hundred cats cheered and Duchess smiled. Now she could have her grand coming-out ball, and naturally the strange debonair cat would be her date.

Lady cats around the country heard the true story of Duchess and how she passed the test that proved her fine breeding. To this day to prove they are of a pure fine breed, cats periodically stare and pounce at nothing just as Duchess did.

Occasionally stories of Duchess and her latest boy-cats make it into magazines, but because she is now of "proven royalty," the stories are handled nicely. It is what they call specially treated kitty litter.

The Three Little Kitties

 NCE UPON A TIME there were three little kitties all born in the same litter. The first one's name was Kitty. The second one's name was Kitty-Kitty. The third one's name was Kitty-Kitty-Kitty. They looked alike, but because of their different names it was easy to tell them apart.

Eventually, as happens with kitties born of the same litter, it came time for each to set out to seek his fortune and build a little kitty house of his own. So all the kitties set out.

The first Kitty, who preferred playing with his little cat toys to building houses, took the easiest route. He collected some long sweet grasses and before long had a little though somewhat flimsy house all built. He moved in and at once made use of his rumpus room by batting around his collection of little stuffed mice.

Kitty-Kitty, who had a little more sense but not much, decided to see what he could scrounge up from the local lumberyard. Alas, how could a poor little kitty ever carry two-by-fours? Spying some wood shavings, Kitty-Kitty knew his problem was solved. Jumping into the pile of shavings, he collected enough on his fur to build his house and sooner than later there he was in his rather novel but just as flimsy house. Immediately he called over some cats he knew and had a mousy barbe-cue. Then they set to chasing one another around the house, as cats will do for amusement.

Kitty-Kitty-Kitty was different from his brothers. He

was a wise cat gifted with common sense and instinct. He knew that the best house would be one that would last and would keep out natural enemies like dogs and hawks and certain gourmet chefs. He went to the local gravel pit and collected stones. When his brothers were long into playing and entertaining, he was still batting the little stones around, trying to build the first wall. He was a patient cat, however, and was not worried. His kitty house would be sturdy and would surely last forever.

One day what should come creeping around the neighborhood but a dog that looked like a wolf. He was called Wolf Dog and was feared by all. It was obvious to him that this was a neighborhood that had cats living in it. Soon enough Wolf Dog set to sniffing them out so that he could chase them, scare them, and perhaps make a meal or two of them.

He knew that if he disguised himself as a door-to-door salescat, rousting the three little kitties out of their respective houses would be no problem. He would try to coax them out, for he knew that cats did not respond to wild threats. They responded to food.

He spied the little grass house.

"Kitty?" he mewed as best he could, though it was a rather gruff meow. "Let me in and I will tell you of the new food plan I am selling. It is from a local fish hatchery."

Kitty was very afraid of the gruff meow that coaxed him. It certainly did not sound like any door-to-door salescat that he had ever heard.

"Kitty? If you do not come out right now, I will come in and get you," the gruff meow said.

Although Kitty was not quite as wise as Kitty-Kitty-Kitty, he was not quite so dumb as to jump straight into the jaws of danger. Quietly creeping out his back window, he slid down the wall of his little grass house and hid out in a nearby alleyway.

After three hours of coaxing, Wolf Dog realized that Kitty must not be at home any longer, and he set out to find Kitty-Kitty's house, which was not difficult to spot.

"Kitty-Kitty?" he began, figuring for some reason that perhaps this cat would fall for his trick. "Come here and I will tell you about the fish hatchery's delightful food plan that I have come to sell you. It is so delicious!"

Now that is strange, thought Kitty-Kitty. All the time I have been living in this neighborhood I have not heard of a fish hatchery, least of all one with a food plan for cats. "Go away," said Kitty-Kitty. "I do not believe that you are a salescat."

"But, Kitty-Kitty, it is so delicious. Even while I stand here talking to you I am eating some delicious fish. Mmmm." And then he made smacking noises to try to entice Kitty-Kitty.

Kitty-Kitty was no fool, and while Wolf Dog stood there still pitching his ridiculous food plan Kitty-Kitty crept out his back window and down through his wood shavings and scurried off to the alleyway to hide with his brother Kitty.

Now Wolf Dog was becoming angry. He could not find the delectable Kitty or Kitty-Kitty, and he was getting hungry for his dinner.

What should he chance upon next but the stone house of Kitty-Kitty-Kitty. Although all but three walls were finished, Wolf Dog, both ferocious and polite, stood at the front door.

"Kitty-Kitty-Kitty? Come to your door and I will tell you of my new food plan. I am from the local fish hatchery." And once again he smacked his lips in hopes of enticing poor Kitty-Kitty-Kitty. Needless to say, it did not work at all with Kitty-Kitty-Kitty. Quicker than lightning Kitty-Kitty-Kitty ran out the back of his house, which was not difficult to do at all. Scurrying off to the alleyway, he also hid—right next to his brothers Kitty and Kitty-Kitty.

Wolf Dog took off in search of these three evasive cats. Perchance you have heard him in your neighborhood, for he is not to be seen.

Late at night poke your head out your door and listen. You will hear him call in a gruff voice that is trying to sound like a cat, calling, "Kitty? Kitty-Kitty? Kitty-Kitty-Kitty?" Then he will make smacking noises with his lips, obviously still trying to sell them his food plan.

Kittyunzel

 NCE UPON A TIME, long ago and far away, lived a poor bewitched lady cat. Her name was Kittyunzel.

Early during her kittyhood Kittyunzel had been poking around in her yard when all of a sudden—*zap!*—she managed to get in the way of a curse that one witch was flinging at another witch. Thus poor Kittyunzel ended up with a curse that, first, sent her flying through the air to live in a tower and, second, was such that for as long as she lived in the tower, her coat would grow and grow and grow.

Poor Kittyunzel. Day in, day out in her tower she sat, not even knowing that she was a cat anymore because when she looked in the mirror she never saw a cat, she saw a bunch of hair.

One day a rather adventurous cat named Tom Cat— a common name for adventurous, well-traveled cats— heard of Kittyunzel's plight and immediately set out to save her.

Sure enough, soon he spied her tower. He knew that it was hers because of the enormous hair balls that were strewn about the yard. "As large as casaba melons!" Tom exclaimed. He was known for his descriptive ability. Sitting at the foot of the tower, he howled:

"Kittyunzel! Kittyunzel! Let down your hair
That I may climb your overgrown stair!"

Kittyunzel perked up her ears. She had been alone in her tower so long that she knew not what was howling at her. Nevertheless she obliged, and immediately an enormous mound of cat hair landed on Tom.

Tom scampered up her coat and crept in through the tower window.

"Kittyunzel, I have come to save you!" he mewed proudly.

"Screeeech! What are you?" Kittyunzel said.

"Why, I am a cat! An adventurous cat! A handsome cat! A brave cat! A tomcat. A . . ."

"Very impressive, but what's a cat?"

"Cat? C-a-t? The first word you learned to spell in school?"

"I never went to school. I got *zapped* early in life and have since been in this tower."

"Me-oh," mewed Tom, thinking for a moment. "Well, what do *you* think you are?" She certainly does have a problem, he thought.

"An unzel."

"A what?"

"An unzel, for if I were a cat, I would be called Kitty-

Cat, like Tom Cat, or Pussy Cat, et cetera. I am Kitty Unzel."

"Oh, my poor Kittyunzel," howled Tom. "Surely, had you known that you were a cat, you would have saved yourself from your plight long ago!"

"Me-how?" meowed Kittyunzel.

"By jumping."

"Screeech! What do you mean 'jumping'? You crazy cat, climbing my overgrown coat just to . . ."

"Now listen to me, Kittyunzel," purred Tom, trying to calm her down. "You are a *cat*. Trust me—a real kitty *cat*. 'Unzel' is . . ." Tom did not know what it was. "'Unzel' is just a thing."

"Me-oh . . ." purred Kittyunzel, more or less understanding.

"Now about this 'jumping'—since you are a cat, you can jump from great heights and you will land on your feet."

"No! I know that if I do as you say I will surely become flattened. Other cats will look at me and say,

'Oh, look! There's Kittyunzel, that bitty kitty, that squashed unzel, that flat cat, that . . ."

"Not to worry," said Tom as he headed for the window. "As a cat you have nine lives. If you mess up on the first jump, you have eight more tries left." Tom quickly did a mental calculation to add up his leftover lives. "So leap to your feet, Kittyunzel, and henceforth you shall be free from this tower and free from your abundant furry coat!"

And sure enough! Both Tom Cat and Kittyunzel leaped from the tower window, paw in paw, and both landed gracefully on their feet on the first try. They married at once and lived happily ever after for the rest of their multitudinous lives.

Pinokitty

NCE UPON A TIME in a land in another country lived a cat who was into wood. Why was he into wood? you may ask. Well, it all began one day when he took to scratching at his scratching post and discovered that he could make beautiful wood scratchings if he kept at it long enough. So he did.

Day after day Gepekitty would scratch and scratch at the bits of wood that he imported. He had bits of teak from far away India; bits of American pine from Bangor, Maine; and bits of gumwood tree from Australia. Granted, the gumwood was a little hard to work with, but Gepekitty found that he could really stretch his talents if he stuck with it long enough. He was truly a master craftscat.

One day Gepekitty woke up as usual and ran to his dish. He then jumped into his little box and dug around a bit. Then he cleaned his little paws, patted down his coat, and twiddled his whiskers. In short he began another average day.

"I am lonely," he mewed. He realized that although this average day was not a particularly *bad* day, it was not a particularly *good* day, for he was indeed lonely. He stared at the wall for a moment and thought. Then he jumped.

"*Eurekat!*" he howled and immediately set about scratching up a storm. He used his best wood, his best hide glue, and his best bits of yarn and string. "I will make a puppet!" Then he thought, "No! I will make a *cat*pet! It will be a little wooden cat for me to play with."

When his little wooden cat was almost finished, Gepekitty fashioned a little snout out of gumwood and stuck it to the little wooden cat's face. Then he said, "Henceforth I shall call you Pinokitty, for although that is a strange name for the average cat, it is a good name for you."

All of a sudden Pinokitty began to jump and dance as only a little wooden cat could. Needless to say, Gepekitty was ecstatic. He had scratched out lots of four-legged wooden things before—chairs, tables, television stands—but none of them had ever jumped and danced.

"You must be magic!" meowed Gepekitty.

"No," answered Pinokitty. "I can move because you love me—and also because you are jiggling my strings."

"Welcome to my house," mewed Gepekitty. "From this day forth we shall live in happiness."

All went well for a while. Gepekitty would work all day, and Pinokitty would play all day. Gepekitty did not

mind this arrangement, for he figured Pinokitty was but a young wooden cat and therefore should be allowed to play all day.

One day, however, Pinokitty decided, as only a cat with sawdust for brains could, that he wanted to run away for a while to see how real tomcats play. He crept out of the woodshop window.

On the way down the drainpipe what should he see but a floating cat with blue eyes and blue hair.

"I am the Blue Hairy," it said. "You can go out this time to learn about life, and I will protect you. But if you should lie to Gepekitty when you return, your snout will grow!" Then it vanished.

"Hmph," snorted Pinokitty. What did he know of floating cats?

Sure enough, Pinokitty, blockhead that he was, ran amok while running with his tomcat friends.

First he sought out delicacies in a trash can. Alas, he fell in and howled for hours before a misdirected shoe hit the can instead of him, tipping it and releasing him.

He heard his tomcat friends tell tales of the giant rats that got away and decided to chase one of these giant rats for himself. Unfortunately it turned out to be a giant dog (for what did he know of rats?), and it chased him instead.

Lastly he listened with ardor as his tomcat friends told of a local restaurant that served cats. Spiffing himself up, he set out to visit this restaurant to see if he could get served. Alas, he almost did get served and narrowly escaped, losing several hairs from his tail as he ran.

Three days later poor Pinokitty found his way home. He was a mess.

"Where have you been?" screeched Gepekitty, for he had been very worried. Poor Pinokitty, relying on misinformation from his tomcat friends as to what to say, answered: "Nowhere." And immediately his snout grew.

Gepekitty, who knew that certain wood, when left out for several nights, could warp, thought little of this.

"What do you mean 'nowhere'? What have you been up to?"

"Nothing." And once again, more snout.

"Well then," continued Gepekitty, giving Pinokitty one last chance to explain, "if you have been nowhere, and you have been up to nothing, you must have a good reason for straying. Why are you three days late in getting home?"

"I had a flat tire," mewed Pinokitty, and immediately his snout grew to an enormous length. He no longer looked like a little wooden cat. He looked like an anteater.

Gepekitty sighed, for though he had thought of putting rubber wheels on Pinokitty instead of paws, he hadn't done it, and, alas, he knew that Pinokitty had lied.

Gepekitty realized that it was not good for a little wooden cat to play all day and decided to give Pinokitty a job to do. Nowadays Pinokitty hangs around the woodshop snorting termites while Gepekitty pulls strings to keep him working.